A Certain Forgiveness

Poems by
Carol Kapaun Ratchenski

Winner of The Birdy Poetry Prize—2019

by Meadowlark Books

A Certain Kind of Forgiveness

A MEADOWLARK BOOK

Meadowlark (an imprint of Chasing Tigers Press)
meadowlark-books.com
P.O. Box 333, Emporia, KS 66801

Cover Photo by Kevin Zepper.
Author Photo by Taylor Made Photography.

ISBN: 978-1-7322410-5-3

Library of Congress Control Number: 2019904949

For my great loves. You are my teachers.

Also, please forgive me.

Contents

What is infinite, it appears,

what is always imaginable,

always subject to analysis,

adventure, and creation is past time.

-Toni Morrison

Lifesavers

Free needles and free condoms and free composition
books. Lifesavers all. A decent fast writing pen. Wide
lines and a hard cardboard back. Any nine by thirteen
will do. Space enough to allow complexity, to blow apart
the last couplet. Enough time to rewind it all, to keep
believing in the deep unbroken interior rhyme of my
grandfather's lyric. Sung over whiskey, in blizzards, next
to coffins. Sad and sustaining, true as cranberries in the
Fall. Sugar unnecessary. Sweet promise of a juice stain
warm as French wine. Warm as beer in Berlin. Stout,
intoxicating, sure of itself the way no poet over thirty is.
Humility between broken lines with falling plot lines.
And Mary Oliver still out there, writing, hiking, calling
her dog home to the fire, to soup and bread and cheese.
Comfort of a sunset. Rest coming soon enough. Always
time for a nap, a country western song in four-four time
sits right next to a pristine haiku which sits right next to
my grandmother's bitter nettle tea. Sweet and poignant.
A pen behind your ear, safe and available as the surf at
dawn. Also, more dangerous.

Looking

In junior high it feels like envy. Beautiful underwear, Olga, with lace around the legs and waist in colors so soft they hurt my eyes, baby blue, pale green, pink. Richer girls, more popular girls, pastel girls, blonde, straight hair. I couldn't stop looking.

Sitting in a circle of women, I am almost thirty. It feels like jealousy. I want to be like her. Boyish, playful, sharp edges, and flowing too. I want to be her, wear only one earing, stop shaving my legs, wear my hair short and red, laugh easily, out loud, even at myself. I read the books she recommends and compliment her poetry though it is awful. I couldn't stop looking.

A predictable life at thirty-five, a husband, a child, family pictures on the wall. It feels like choking. Couple friends and game nights and movies in bed, buttered popcorn scenting our high thread count sheets. I can't stop looking away, far off, anywhere else.

Train trip, monastery, silent retreat. It feels like home. Shaved heads, saffron robes, hips sway, fingers touch. A nightly talk: the dharma, the sanga, how to live and how to sit and how to breathe. I am forty-five. I am a girl and so are you. I am hungry. I eat rice. I am reaching over tea. I am praying to Buddha, I am crying to Jesus. I can't stop looking at you.

Changes

I walk around
and around and around
and around and
around.

Still it's a cemetery
still it's a river
it keeps flowing
keeps growing.

My walking
my stillness.
Changes nothing
every time.

Changes everything
every day going
around and around
and around.

Lose memory
gain my footage.
Float above it all
somedays.

It's just a cemetery
just a river
just a woman
just one path to travel.

Me a
traveler
you the tide,
us the undertow.

*It's so hard to love people who hurt and disappoint you, but those
are the only kind of people there are.*
-C.G. Jung

Coffee and Lies

Coffee isn't supposed to taste good.
That's why we shield our children from it

Something to grow into, to wait for
an adult mystery that
something could be so loved and so bitter.
Try the yellow, the pink, the old fashioned cube
still, black truth on my mouth
full fat cream only makes it last longer
deep like dirt
dark like night
unknown dreams of teeth and hair
something to hold
proof in this round planet
all its suns and moons
just out of sight
but never silent or pure or still.

Deeply

I am startled by the swing of his hips as he walks off the stage and back again for an encore. The sway of bad knees that shows up farther north and also south. He is unfamiliar to me without his sweaty bandana, sculpted arms, flat stomach, torn Levi's, boots. I come to the show for his straight up Wild Turkey masculinity—a bass carrying the melody line. His voice lands in my chest, so utterly other that the world's balance rights itself a little. Voice of gravel. Unkempt, and holy. A woman in a black slip makes room for lyrics about grandchildren, gardens, a body stooping in the wind. Softer, older, concerned with decades past. A tiny little future to consider, a great big past to regret, to rewrite. Ten years older than I am, the same age as my last boy lover, who was with me the last time I heard the singer sing. My lover did not enjoy him, too crabby and insincere and ungrateful he said. One more reason to leave him in Wisconsin or at least not to cry when he leaves me somewhere on the highway west. This memory like a shot of coke to my head. Loving boys, holding boys, wishing boys would talk about their feelings until they do. The demands of counter sex, hopes of symmetry and completion. The ways we overlook each other, threaten each other, hate each other along the throbbing roads not taken. It's his lyrics, so right, so unexpected and inevitable, but that's a lie too. It's his big feet and square hands, his posture, his stubble, his socks, his stare. The freedom of not being seen that sits in the middle of opposite sex love affairs. Unquestioned, unexamined, mysterious, accepted withholding and unknowing, a rich, dark, reliable glue.

Storm Warning

All my relationships like

a drive in bad weather
ill thought out
dangerous
never sure if we should
keep going
I'm steering (but not really)
in zero visibility
wind and ice
so little control of this thing
that outweighs me
by so much.

Still the roadside
blueberries
sweet and purple
and hopeful
a horizon of
sunflowers
the mother ball of fire
herself
resting on these flat plains
yellow
blinding heads of life
unspeakably sure of themselves.

Our shared destinations
destinies and wildest dreams
merge together
one big surprise party
called life.
Something to help us remember
why we came
and the bitterness too
cruel and unpredictable

a blur out the
passenger window
shapeless and foggy.

We came
for this
we'll never know
why we came at all
settle for a few chapters
of strong plot
and a good AM signal
agree to ignore the
hourly road reports
for something
under water somewhere
in a tornado watch
somewhere we
visited last summer
reminders still
in our trunk
driftwood
and blue green
sea glass.

Sing Out Bob, Loud

My friend saw him at the Purple Onion. My sister's husband was at Woodstock, amongst the betrayed and disillusioned, before Vietnam showed him what a broken promise really feels like. I saw him in a football stadium, a memory blurred by pot smoke and inaudible wisdom. Loud and mean and ungrateful truths in rhyme and meter. The predictable, stunning magic of four-four time. All that haze foretelling another purple magician who would romance us with boas and something to say both loud and mysterious, soft and quiet. These two Minnesotans so unlike the rumored masses: straight forward, obvious, understated across generations of unvoiced screams. Injustice and sex and ecstasy, muffled on these northern plains, under down comforters and fields of barley, corn and sweet alfalfa. Here, lakeside or near the western valley, we live with the kind of winter that makes us all poets or crazy, often both. We need their ideals and their violence. We know our children will need to learn how to lose, how to grieve, how to let go, how to bury us young and how to love us anyway. So we argue and we judge. We pray for rain and settle for a generous raspberry crop. We crave forgiveness and we dance in church basements and VFW's, in laundry rooms and sunflower fields. When he turned sixty we couldn't believe it. When we knew he never would we couldn't believe it too.

Reverse Magic

Poetry is a counter spell
call on it
it will break trance
it will wake you up
in a dream
you are a song lyric,
and my teeth are falling out.
Elevators go to the wrong
floor every time
all night long.

Poetry is scaffolding like
rope and cedar,
tofu and silk,
Atwood and Walker
Allende, Angelou and Alexie.
knots of Mary
and Martha and
the other Mary.
Judas and Jesus.

Poetry for all the
fishermen who kept on fishing
who did not follow or
drop everything
but believed in flannel
and fennel and clove
turmeric and honey
fiction is always true
one quilt two mugs
untold stories.

In my lover I need
someone who needs me
someone who
knows when to touch

and when to stay away.
I trust the dark
stairwell
and the ink
and the charcoal.
Truth is found in a
a chorus that rhymes
with an old memory of mine.

Poetry is a counter-spell
it won't bring you back
it won't unsay what I regret
saying.
Still I count on it,
I cling to it,
I crave it.
A reversal of all that
has harmed anyone that I loved.
Make every slap a kiss
make everything rhyme
with there, there.
There, there.

Love Many Things

I'm new
I like dirt
and the color green
and fuzzy warm milk, big hands
harps
the smell of mother, vanilla and mint
rocking and stretching and yawning.

I'm young
I like knives and roller coasters
gravel roads
fireworks and feeling scared
adrenaline and hot pepper flakes and graveyards
the smell of sex, moonlight and noise.

I'm in the middle
I don't know where to look
so much behind me
buried alive under my feet
I don't like anything
I'm grieving and restless and clinging.

I'm old
I like soft things
large vocabularies in men
strong straight teeth in women
honey and sidewalks and clean laundry on the line
lilies, rainstorms, children, evergreen trees.

I'm letting go
I like wind and lemon pie
worn out towels and flannel sheets
feather pillows, cardinals, and all the empty space
between my thoughts
laughing and crying and forgetting.

Mess

It's a city. It's a mess.
We are a family.
We don't share one
memory.
Except this:
Everyone died too young.
At fifty-two
at sixty-three
at ninety-four.
Goddamn she almost
made it to ninety-five.
Unfinished lives
everywhere,
unsure with no
conclusion, spinning
Earth-like, in trust
that every wave reaches
somewhere
and anywhere is as
good as anywhere else.

So I get up earlier
than I need to and write
poetry and go to sleep
on poetry that I refuse
to capture, write down.
Surely a sin on my part,
but I will not begin
the morning with no,
rather yes to the verse
in my head
coming awake barely aware
is it raining or sunny
are you here with me
disembodied lines

no bitter food image yet attached
to awaken in my reader
his mouth, her heart
some urge to live longer
some desire to reach out
like all decent verse will
tidy up a world.

Funeral Date

My sister's birthday and not the anniversary of my
father's funeral. Her selfish request is decades old, faded
and worn out now. It's a big family. Try to avoid dying
on anyone's birthday or three days before or the night
after. Not easy, not possible. Let the roulette wheel spin,
keep your grubby greedy hands off it. Do not grab at
fate. It turns, it stops, it will. You are part of the wheel.
You are on the wheel but you are not the wheel. Not the
owner, or the master or the spinner. The wheel rules
itself, and you and me. We ride it, try to love it,
surrender to it. His funeral will be on your birthday, yes
forever. That is true. Only bad fate can interrupt good
fate, not your wishes, your anger, your need or your
frailty. It is supposed to take a lifetime to trust the red
numbers, to enjoy the ride, to realize something akin to
trust, leaning a little toward resignation. It's a spinning
rattle noise, not music, not a symphony or a quartet or a
silly folk chorus we all know but don't remember
learning. It is my sister's birthday a day after the
anniversary of my father's funeral mass. A lasting
marriage of black iris and white rose.

No Kissing

There will be no kissing in Mexico
though it is deep winter where we travel from
to white sand open blue water
crab legs over sand fires
sticky sweet drinks, grass skirts at the fair.

There will be no kissing on New Year's Eve
though we and our children are healthy
the year has been kind and interesting and prosperous
the wine is expensive
no one is expecting us anywhere.

There will be no kissing on my birthday
I turn fifty as you turn away
friends gather, music plays on the patio
dancing and singing and wishing
packages of chocolate, sketch paper, red wine.

There will be no kissing in Hawaii
it's a wedding at sundown, a picture
a line of couples side by side
"Now everybody kiss," says the photographer
you miss my cheek, my lips, my chin.

There will be no kissing
on dance floors in hot tubs on beaches in cars.
No kissing in showers water falls claw footed tubs.
No love no sweat no gasping no hoping no soar.
No kissing good luck goodnight or goodbye.

Produce and Spice

I'm doing the marketing today

Her hips are tired and her hair's a mess
not herself she's simply unable these days
her spirit diminished, her energy scarce
she made a list, asked that I let her rest.

That's why I'm doing the marketing today.

I don't know the way around
or the butcher's name or how many pounds
sausage, pork, some soup meat, and some starch
we no longer deny she's losing ground.

The marketing is mine to do today.

Also the gutters need to be cleaned
the fallen leaves gathered
our bikes put away
with the golf clubs and camper.

Still the marketing needs doing more than all this.

I long for her old hungry self
planning meals and snacks and breakfast
for all of us who came when she called
us to dinner to lunch to attention to love.

The market was her boardroom, her toolbox and joy.

Tonight she won't remember if she remembered to pee
all day or if her hair needs washing or dying
when I get home I'll ask
when she remembers to look at me.

The marketing is mine to do today
because she still belongs to me.

Women Prefer Wine

It's a Bob Dylan whine
and Cass Elliot's swinging hips
next door.
A brown bottle, purple and pink
melted wax
the way I arch away from the
ripples of not knowing
what to do next.
Your smooth unblemished face,
our hesitation, our questions our
shared fear of the color red.
There are waves and seagulls
a moody rosé like carbonated
heartache.
A toast to me, to you, to us,
to the sea, to a new leaf.
one gulp, one burning sip
spilled down the front of my
blue muslin lace.
We argue for the sake of it,
we reach for each other
by habit, in pattern, in need.
The maroon merlot
is my yearning, the slow pour
into my wide mouthed green glass.
I'm mournful, you're cloudy.
We smell like deep sleepy sex
or the dying lilacs on my
father's grave.
Something old, but breathing
still and tender and
just a little unruly
tide in and tide out.
Crisp, chilled and hopeful,
though the beach is empty

the moon half full
silk and linen against
my legs and chest.
I am a woman reaching
for your knowing and not knowing.
The year matters
the bouquet matters,
particular oval blue grape
is equal parts sour and sweet.
We pretend in our dreams.
The San Joaquin Valley
isn't a real desert.
Too wide, too giving,
too full of liquid desire
dry sand
repetitive dreams
wrong names and
dances that never end.

Dark and Red

Latin American fiction
because it's sticky and heated
a grandfather chained to a tree
chocolate running down her legs
ghosts who sing in Latin
at a communion rail that bursts into flames.

South of the equator
original in Spanish
my northern heart knows to crave this
colorful full skirts
stone houses painted pastel and shuttered
full brows, barrel chests, dark soft warm men.

Below navels and under a red moon
drumming, yearning, coffee with chilies
thorny flora, olives and opium
a different season, an upside down calendar
my stomach settles at last
around everything I want.

Pampering

I have never been to Las Vegas or ridden in a limousine.
I am oddly prideful about both of these random facts.
Also only one professional pedicure, because it was my
friend's bridal shower and not on my credit card or
conscience. Over lunch my young adult nieces compare
their favorite nail spas, cost, gentleness, color selection,
chair comfort. Brown women at their feet. Pampering
substituting for pleasure, play, adventure, entertainment,
joy, hobby, love. Seven years into his cancer journey, our
"family success story," my sister reminds me, the
average survival time back then was only three, my dad
told me that Americans spend more money annually on
nail polish than on cancer research. Stunning, true,
denial, powerlessness. Girls age five, age eleven, age
seventy-seven search shiny rows of color seeking
happiness through beauty. It's not plastic surgery, it's
not even all that costly. Not my point, I slurp with the
end of my sweet tea. I was going to be playful, neutral,
lighthearted, accepting of my painted sisters. Joining
even. Soon to the west, the sun begins to set, sinks into
its quilts of ruby, orange and blue and violet. The orange
reminds me of my mother's favorite nail color, though
she is cancer dead for more than three decades. When
did we agree that human girl bodies simply arrive too
hairy, too soft, too smelly, too moist, too pale, too dark,
too flat, too round, too human. Shiny, unruly, noisy,
smart. What if thread count doesn't matter, and luxury is
not freedom or power or strong or free. What if we are
never comfortable or glamorous or special. We are
simply and only flesh and blood at ninety-eight degrees,
give or take. Each of us will see ten thousand purple-
orange sunsets, maybe less, unlikely more.

Dying Stars

I danced with my lover at her wedding. I cried when her sister couldn't or wouldn't come. She cooks, I bring salad, dessert, real whipped cream over raspberries, or pie or a cobbler for four. We watch the years flow over us. More wrinkles, old lovers reappear, we can't remember if we have read that novel or not or just saw a movie trailer that reminded us of it in some distant yearning way. On her birthday I bring cake and the right number of candles, though they cover the top and sprout from the side like wildly independent sparklers on the fourth of July. A waxy mess, strong coffee, Kahlua, piñata. She kneels on the ground picking up the airplane-sized vodka and whiskey bottles splayed by her strikes. She is too close to the fire, maybe drunk, her pants slide down revealing too much. I grab her, others call to her, be careful, step back, watch your hair, watch your sweater. Out of the corner of my eye I see her husband look on without expression, sees her falling and sees me seeing. Then he looks up at the night sky, clear, alive, sparkling with the lying light of so many dead stars.

Alice Walker Told Me

No one can take anything away that has been danced.
My grandmother's red patent leather pumps.
My grandfather's worn bass drum pedal.
My mother's orange fingernails.
My father's stained white goose hunting overalls.

Anything we love can be saved.
My first husband's college sweatshirt.
My second husband's silk striped pajamas.
Your wooden incomplete scrabble board.
Rumpus coffee mug and brass tea strainer.

Nothing is stronger than a circle.
Of stone of steel of yarn of rope of apples.
Of green leather chairs.
Of candles of children of prisoners of priests.
Of the lonely the grateful the ill the departed.

To change the world you must not be afraid of the poor.
Or dark alleys, or skinny boys and girls, thinning hair
and blood in your sweet tea.
Their empty eyes and bright blue dreams.
All the ways they remind you of you.

Martyrs never regret what they have done.
The ropes the dragging the trees the late prayers.
The sureness the questions the pleading mothers.
The history books the mythologies the rumors the deeds.
The failures the mountain tops the sunsets the screams.

The universe belongs to everyone.
The babies in limbo the toothless the mighty.
The hopeless the healers the stragglers the wise.
The sages the singers the dying.
The silly the ugly the stooped and the framed.

Garlic

My mother was allergic to garlic. Or maybe not. Maybe she didn't like garlic or it made her belch. My lover tells restaurant servers that she is allergic to onion. But she isn't. She doesn't like onions and they take her so much more seriously if she says she is allergic. Render images of hives and soft pink throat tissue closing in on itself. I love garlic and onions, such generous bulbs each of them. And adaptive. Hardly claiming anything for themselves. Seldom a main course. Rarely a soup or soufflé. Always the backup singer to the flashy front protein or green. To have fresh garlic and several kinds of onions on hand is to feel rich and full of possibility, which is the same thing. A perfect winter omelet, a long green stem on a Roquefort salad, beside a morel mushroom, a dandelion leaf. My mother is so unknown to me that I cling to this silly fact or lie. She loved lobster and was allergic to garlic. Two gastronomical truths or not. All my mistrust of her is there. I wonder if her throat would collapse at meeting garlic mashed yams, or roasted dark magic floating in thick potato leek soup. If I do not shudder at this deadly, pureed image, what is there for me in an old photograph, her death date anniversary, her still full wallet, old Kleenexes in a coat pocket. Things my father says she said about me. Twenty-seven varieties of onions grow around my garage and I love you both, mother, lover. I smell all that's expected of me as I study you. Your red clay arms, your breath of lemon grass and seaweed. All your requests for my attention that I lean into. The way you cook beside me like a slow dance, our own smoke flavoring a stew and our wet sheets.

Ghosts Of Killdeer

As soon as the gravel road turned
from grey to red
my grandmother was happy
suddenly singing to the radio
dreaming of riding or roping
of her brothers
of Sunday afternoon sunburns
of home.
Like a midnight raid, marriage
had uprooted her
tossed her into town
my grandfather's bed and
ill-fated businesses
and a restlessness that she tried
to believe didn't rhyme with
hopelessness.

A Certain Kind of Forgiveness—Part I

There is a certain kind of forgiveness between mothers and daughters that fathers cannot understand. A certain kind of blue glass shard. A black cohosh root tea. Honey withheld. The sour turn of a morning glance over a chipped cup. Dark roast. Four sisters one room. Two sisters one bed. Some dreamy grasping, a push into the closet door at midnight. The hidden whiskey. A shared secret. Luke warm water, copper healing, burnt throats and an old story told only between them. A boat, a shotgun. Unquiet houses of the mid-century middle classes. Radios turned to baseball and winter weather warnings. Language of regret, sarcastic and muttered over the din of a moaning refrigerator, a whistling teakettle, a crying baby, a swearing father, a sighing mother. The latter the loudest. All this and still I want to be exactly like her, as beautiful, as fragile, as soft and round and powerful.

A Certain Kind of Forgiveness—Part II

There is a certain kind of
forgiveness between mothers
and daughters that
sons cannot understand.
So I forgive
my mother for hating herself
for weighing herself
girdling herself
wishing herself away
until she left
young and mad and beautiful
barely wrinkled
tragic with no grey hair.
The ways she shunned
her curves and all
soft tissue,
the lining of my heart
my sister's inner thigh
and my grandmothers chin.
I forgive her
for not dancing
not hugging
not squeezing
not smiling
not living
for not having a body
to call my home.

His Story

When my son tells his story
will I be there to hear it
will I recognize it at all
will I be the villain
the madwoman the
dark one the hopeless one
Will he be the hero
the tragic god with no wings
When he tells his story
will I be near
will he be kind
will he credit my grandfather
and my sisters
Will he blame my mother
Will he forget
to mention the ghosts
surely responsible
and innocent beyond clouds
When my son tells his story
what will he leave out
and what will he embellish
to make someone fall in love
to fill the mirror with color
with hope with memory
but not quite.
When my son tells his story
I must remember it is his
bless it and love it and accept it.
Never argue with him
Never edit or correct him
even a little bit.

Son Sounds

My son is twenty-two
I miss the sound of his voice
and the demands for my attention
and the calls for water and juice in the night
I miss his four-year-old self
and his teenaged self
and all the ways he is like me and unlike me
I miss the sound of his voice
swearing under his breath
begging his girlfriend on the phone
cheering on his Xbox football team
shrieks of joy and groans of defeat
his love of snow and thick socks
I miss the sound of his voice
moaning in his sleep
Sunday afternoon
what's for dinner and why can't I go
I miss his march though elementary school
high school taller, more sure
also more to worry about
missed curfews
sex and broken hearts
I miss the sound of his voice
saying anything
explaining anything
asking anything
saying mom
I miss the sound of his voice
the wind the sea
Bach and Dillon and Lennon
church bells
carols and taps
I miss the sound of my son.

What I'm Trying to Get Back To

What I'm trying to get back to is
new work boots every other year
dress shoes once a decade
jitterbugging
fresh flowers from the yard.

What I'm trying to get back to is
frozen pizza Friday nights
weekly prime time TV schedules
new pajamas
Grandma and Jesus too.

What I'm trying to get back to is
summer humid nights forever
root beer floats
throwing something to the dog
golf balls, and frisbees.

What I'm trying to get back to is
glass bottles of soda and beer
front porches, candidates to love
purple lilacs
card tricks with iced tea.

What I'm trying to get back to is
push lawn mowers and snow shovels
sunday mass, stations of the cross
the rosary
forgiveness that's never been for sale.

What I Miss About Boys

car care
few tears
heavy lifting
acquiescence
firm reaching
a king size bed
clear desire
(easy satisfaction)
concrete thinking
baseball
grill skill
thick hands
flattery
meatloaf and gravy
few tears
dirty jokes
deep sleep
fur and stubble
boats
trucks
tractors
tee time
black coffee
whiskey
habaneros
Motown
my tears

What I Miss About Girls

flannel
honey
a shade of pink
coffee with cream
read to me
tea with sugar
sameness
a shared thirst for jazz
silk everything
listening
eyelashes
porches
shared Levi's
confessing it all
manners
harmonies
soups, stews
a park at dusk
hips
wine
soft and
softer
afternoon naps
silence
habaneros
our tears
mirrors

A Certain Kind of Forgiveness—Part III

There's a certain kind of forgiveness between mothers and daughters that grandchildren can't understand. I have three sons. They are each an only child. Lonely, stubborn, self-absorbed, and unwilling to care for each other. Their lives don't touch they tell me. Three sons, separate and yet my friends can't tell them apart on the street. Tall and dark and square, different fathers, same sturdy build. No wonder they can tell themselves they don't need each other, need anyone. No fear in being a white, square man. Until terror moves in. Never where expected or predicted. The winter storm out of Canada, the levee that does break against all odds and engineering. With a pop, with a thud, with a holy charm only a mother could appreciate.

Poetry

It broke his heart
he loved it most.
The lonely whine
steel guitar
microphone buzz
delicate harmony
interior rhyme
typewriter and
broken piano
keys
omelets
seafood stews
red rock salt and
white pepper flour.
Blue underground
light and dark
morel mushrooms
spider dreams
webs of luck
and longing
communion wine.
He wrote he read
he wrote he taught
he read he edited
he taught he wrote
he read
he loved it most.
Broken wings
bluegrass tunes
songs that won't
leave your head.
it broke his heart.
He loved it most.

Fur

I wrote a poem last week about what I miss about boys.
There was one line I could not get right, draft after draft,
craving an embodied image, a visceral line. Everything
too sentimental, obvious or false. Until fur and stubble.
It says, "he used to keep my car full of gas and clean, oil
changed Saturday mornings before I woke up." That's
not the important part but it's not the least of it either.
When I go out for sushi with my son tonight, he will
pick me up and his pickup will be warm and he will turn
the rap music off before my door closes. I won't
mention the smell of cigarettes and he won't light up
when we drive. We'll order our favorites and laugh at all
the family news that warrants it and some that doesn't.
His cousins, their boyfriends, what are they thinking?
He'll remind me to pay his tuition and I'll remind him to
put his gloves on. It's a long walk from here. We don't
need these reminders but they comfort me. He wants a
new kind of governance from congress and a freedom
that I know isn't for sale, in fact is the opposite of for
sale, but I can't remember the word for that. An end to
capitalism seems possible to him. His youth raw and
reaching like his ambitions and dreams, the books he's
reading and the books he's refusing to read. The books
I'm writing and the books I can't find time to read. The
ways we collide in the prose of Sherman Alexie and the
poetry of James Merrill and the suspense of Breaking
Bad and Jeopardy! All answers in the form of questions.
I trust these thin threads of commonality like our shared
allergies to mint and penicillin. All his next steps
cooking on high. My plans simmering on low. I'm not
wishing for big change. I'm dreaming of long life and
grandchildren. He rolls his eyes and tells me he wants a
dog. In his hope and sarcasm I recognize an old flannel
shirt and the sparking need for nicotine. His father and
myself.

Borderlands

Borderlands are tender and sacred and most often unbeautiful. The times I have gone to the Yucatan and lost myself and the times I have gone to Manhattan and looked for you. Absurd, I know. But my grandmother told me that even Moscow is just a bunch of neighborhoods put together, one after another, sometimes on top of each other. She could have saved the world a lot of trouble if she had more important listeners than me and my sisters. She knew why wedding dances and funeral processions feel the same if you close your eyes. I looked around the edges of the theater district and at Rockefeller Center, though I knew that was too cliché, too Russian, too romantic which is the same thing. Hell's Kitchen and Queen's, barbershops and bus stations, subway stairways, Eastern Europe newsstands and Hungarian delis. Chalk outlines always remind me of you, tragic, transitory, always the performer. The borderlands of middle age are broad and unspeakable, memories of blood and expectation. Grief has become the mainland, and the equator and the moon. My borderlands are fuzzy and disputed and necessary. Decades away from the ambitions and compromises and friends of my youth. Over there yesterday, over there last summer, all our plans and regrets and need for love live across the invisible divide now. Reassigned and still on fire.

Reasons

You are a pile of yellowed reasons, tattooed on my wrist
and you are the green leather tattoo artist's table I laid
down on and faced east for luck and received pain. Of
course it all made sense once. Reading *One Hundred Years
of Solitude* out loud to each other in bed, writing on the
walls of your grandfather's barn. My lifelong sensory
association: manure of horses fed on sweet grass,
orgasm. Horseback riding and running. I dropped you
off twelve miles from home, then me behind the wheel
of your red International pickup truck, pretending I
knew how to drive a manual transition, you never
mentioning that I clearly didn't. Me waiting in the
driveway, you smelling that way and your damp lips
grabbing my neck. Sometimes you wore saran wrap
under your grey sweats if you were struggling to reach
your wrestling weight. When my nephew broke your
high school wins by pin record, I was proud. I don't
know why you are dead, all the reasons too shiny. You
were duck hunting in the badlands: a favorite sport, a
favorite slue, a favorite mare. No branches down, a
gentle fall, a heart attack your mother whispers but she
doesn't look me in the eye. Your green eyes are cloudy,
half closed on her face. Tranquilizers I suppose. It's
October again, red and orange and greedy.
Temperatures like August, northern lights and
campfires, you falling slowly into fallen red and yellow
leaves, no sound to accompany you to the other side of
this life. My faith in this as jerky as the stick shift, as our
young love, as our nakedness and not nearly as true.

Dickey County

With a roll of an eye
under her Merlot breath
an aside to me
"It's the Dickey county thing."

The braided rug
peed on and scrubbed
hanging from the back porch railing
for six months.

More pee
three cats by then
the blended stink of home
we cannot smell.

A fog of habits
cats not dogs,
Democrats, unions, and seasonal
unemployment.

Pinochle, not bridge,
whiskey and poker on Christmas
grandmothers raise grandchildren
when called, no questions asked.

Beds we kneel by
friends we knew in first grade
a family pew
a Bible and a mandolin.

Grandpas who can't say no
to you. And so you
believe in god and angels
and all good things in the night.

Green of Winter

The green of winter is not the yeasty smell of mold. It is not money and it is not green funeral lunch jello. The green of winter is my grandmother feeding her wood stove with broken logs my father and uncle chopped for her and piled in her kitchen every other day. The green of winter is the seed catalog she holds in her mittened hands because she's stingy with the wood in case my uncle stays all night at the casino and forgets that Saturday is his day. Woolen, orange mittens, bought at the local hardware store. Made for deer hunters; she can release her fingertips, not for pulling the trigger, but for a smoke. The green of winter is not a mint julep fancy drink or indoor-outdoor carpeting or a felt-topped pool table. The green of winter is my son dressed in layers and setting up his grandfather's auger to fill an idling grain truck from the silver bin and then driving to the local elevator by noon because miraculously the price of barley went up this morning. The green of winter is not tea with honey or leafy greens sautéed in ghee and ginger. The green of winter is my father's plumbing truck parked in front of St. John's Catholic Church before dawn. The moon and the big dipper silent and watching. Stations of the cross every day of lent, every winter of his life. With his mother, with my mother, alone, no time to stop and hope one of my sisters might join him. The green of winter is not a hopeful shoot of tulip or a college football field or a new year's fireworks display. The green of winter is my belief that you will come back, willing to forget, anxious to forgive, craving my caustic humor and burnt toast with green tomato marmalade, sour and dark and tasting surprisingly like summer in January.

Hometown

No one really cares if you set a bag of wet mittens on
fire. No one really cares if you sing songs about guns
and whiskey on the way to the peace rally. No one really
cares if you regret everything you've ever done,
including love them and lie to them. No one really cares
if you are a size six or a size sixteen. No one really cares
if you give your money away or if you fund your
grandson's habit or your granddaughter's acting career.
No one really cares if you finished *War and Peace* or *Moby
Dick* or if you made the pie from scratch. No one really
cares if you pray five times a day or say the rosary in
traffic. No one really cares if you carry and conceal or if
you duck and cover. No one really cares if you want
sons or beautiful daughters or a new wife. No one really
cares if you still bite your fingernails or sneak a pour in
your morning coffee. No one really cares if you forget to
vote or remember to knock first. No one really cares if
you know the words to Woodie or Mahalia. No one
really cares if you come by with flowers on Memorial
Day or candles on Christmas Eve. No one really cares
unless you don't stay.

Mother Forever

Jessie is finally, hugely, completely pregnant. She stands because she is uncomfortable sitting. Then she sits because she is uncomfortable standing. Then she stands again. She is round and impatient and waiting. Thirty-six weeks along, backache all day, thicker, shiny hair. Her mouth is dry and her feet don't fit in her cowboy boots, even the high gloss grey ones with red stitching that she stole off her grandfather in his redwood coffin, living up to grandma's accusation that he was a dandy, too fancy, living too high, too much always. The girl baby kicking and flopping under Jesse's stretched sweatshirt dress will never know this grandpa, so optimistic, or this grandma, so afraid. Form fitting knit maternity wear is the fashion now. Gone the wide hemmed blouses, sailor collars, and folds of material that even by week forty were never filled in. Fourteen inches of elastic topped pants. Ugly dressing in preparation for days of unwashed hair, damp dresses, yellow diapers. Jesse isn't a first-time mother, but she has never held her new infant up to a Christmas tree, stopped his pudgy hand from grabbing a blue flashing bulb before he can move it to his mouth. She is not a first-time mother, but she has never cried on the first day of kindergarten, swore at fourth grade math homework, or snuggled over to make room for a bad dream in feet pajama, three in the morning, flannel sheets, room to spare. Jesse is studied in infant therapeutic touch, human development over the life span, the delicate transition from concrete operational thinking to abstract thinking. Jesse has read books on inspirational parenting, mindful parenting, parenting as a spiritual path, parenting a spirited child, and how and when to introduce a second language, in song and bedtime stories, where access to the left side of the brain is most available. She stretches, burbs, farts, and blushes, apologizes. Rolls her brown eyes, says, "Oh for fuck's sake. I'm going to spank this baby as soon as she gets out here." A beautiful tangle of love and grief, pain and anticipation: a mother forever.

Dreams

You dream of classrooms you can't find and students who are unknown to you and expecting someone else, a physics professor perhaps or chemistry teacher's assistant. I dream of customers seated at dirty tables, a hostess who forgets to seat anyone in my section, and unpaid tabs that will come out of my tips. My sister dreams of patients who go from ready for discharge to coding and morphine pumps that won't pump and doctors who don't answer their phones.

My brother dreams of broken fishing line and rifles full of blanks and elk running over the hill, into the sun, away forever. My lover dreams of lost passwords and warehouses that forget to deliver and salespersons who undercharge and creditors who come to our house. My mother dreams of pregnant daughters and stained sheets and doctors who can't keep children well. My father dreams of meetings that never end and water heaters that never arrive and his wife kissing his brother on the dance floor.

My grandfather dreams of losing the downbeat and horns that come in sharp and lost mallets and boos from the crowd. My grandmother dreams of underdone turkey and estranged children and funerals of everyone. My son dreams of stalled combines and falling prices and ground too wet, too dry, too late, too early. Seeds that never grow through the black soil. We all wake up sweaty and relieved and sure of so many things that could be worse that might even happen today.

We are all restless we are all anxious we are each tender and harsh and afraid. We are human. We forget how to pray, trust god half the time, easier in the spring and harder in the winter. Still, snow melts and rains stop. Evening falls and the sun rises. Dreams fade and we plan and greet each other through a broken fence.

In A Name

If my name were Daphne
if your name were Alexander
things would have gone
differently
things would have gone
better
You would have begged me
to stay
I would have lied more
and slept longer
and moaned louder.
If my name were Doris
if your name were Edward
we would have tried harder
we would have expected less
we would have prayed
more and taught
our children to
genuflect, to confess, to bow.
If my name were Sarah
if your name were Joseph
I would have been patient
you would have been loyal
we would have been warmer
and more afraid
and closer to my sisters
and your parents
We would have tended a garden
and cleaned the church
on Saturdays after eggs with bacon.
If my name were Helena
if your name were Sam
we would have danced more
you would have cried at the ballet
I would have learned to fish
our children would be musicians

and I would never have cut my hair
You would never have left the room
when I needed you to need me
more than I needed
symphony tickets and new shoes.
My name is Kathy
your name is Daniel
We loved each other we hated each other
we hurt each other
the exact same amount as we
needed each other until
once, we both turned away
and no one called the other
home.

Afraid to Talk About It

By the river
Three big girls
Glitter gowns
Lipstick
Love

Chatter chide
Sounds of thigh
Against thigh
Me not
Afraid

Dinner party
Four couples
And me
War
Ballads playing

So many dead
Children
Shot in
The sand
Bombs

Who is David
And not
Me
Afraid to talk
Grave digging

Israel
Pakistan
Land, rock, blood
Fear
All men

A wedding
Picture this
Three big girls
On the beach
Dead

Four boys
And a ball
By the river
Laughter
Safety

Nighttime
White sheets
Sandy feet
Alive
Damp hair

Playground
Screaming
Posing for
A red future
Soup and bread

The Mother Coast

I have reached the mother coast.
Now you are in the middle
of your second decade
No need for my wake to move you
Your own waves greet you
surprise you and grow you.

From here I can look all ways.
Over there kindergarten
just next to three funerals
in four months
Your misunderstanding
of death and heaven and still
comfort comes your way.

Video games and basketball
and school plays and musicals
and prom and hair dye.
Beer and cigarettes
heartbreak and broken glass
night arguments
girlfriends who cry too much.

Did your daycare provider hit you?
Did you notice that my sisters
preferred your cousins?
Did you miss me when I worked too much?
Did you notice when your dad
began his descent
into a dark bottle, into his own dark heart?

All we didn't talk about
unreachable now, unmentionable now.
Beyond my memory
set aside and adrift to another shore
the lands of what never happened

and all the reasons why
things didn't go as planned.

The mother coast
has no weather
no wind, or moisture or heat.
It is the kind of empty
that might preview hell or Moscow
or Greenland
somewhere unimaginable to us both.

I can look out toward
your children, my fading face
the books we forgot to talk about
the music we didn't agree on
the movies yet to be made
Christmas pageants and disappointment
how we'll visit each other.

I have not stopped missing you.
You have stopped needing me
just when I am settling in at the
Mother coast and need company
and reassurance
I have lost my photographs
and my hope and my regret have taken charge.

Two Men Leaving Me

We once worked in a bookstore
before you were a professor
before I was a therapist
we opened boxes
every day Christmas morning
sniffed the wood pulp and ink
like a drug we couldn't afford yet.

We were married once in a park
in a bandstand in a rainstorm
had children, lost children
found ourselves in the frantic
needs of our separate addictions
we cried and loved
we ran away as fast as we could.

We wrote poetry in coffee shops
and dusty museums and on road trips
your Ford Explorer my VW Bug
every pawn shop our destination
stopping every three hours to pray
because Jesus loves writers
and writers need a god.

We inherited my grandma's silver
your mother's diaries.
We ate with them, we burned them
photos piled up and toys
and resentments and calendars
I grew to hate your friends
you grew to love my sisters.

We drove miles to see Raymond Carver
before he was dead
and Carolyn Forche years too late
agents rejected us

tequila comforted us
also Lorde and Atwood and Alexie
a rare kiss, a small edit in the last stanza.

We find ourselves in our son
and each other too, the best of you
the worst of me all the anxiety of my mother
your father's love of numbers and antique watches
old Chevy pickups and the northern lights
saying goodbye to you both
is like the sky is falling, and everything else too.

Ever After

Life gives us twelve seconds to rehearse
less than the in breath and release
less than a yellow traffic signal
or a quiet teary "I do"
or "Maybe I don't, at least not now"
an exit on the ninth beat
with three to spare, run downstairs
to a car waiting for two
shamelessly noisy with soup cans and
sparklers lit by young impatient nephews
bored with the service inside
madly in love with this mid-century
baby blue Buick transformed into a
rolling Christmas tree.

As the streamers catch fire, the
driver hits the gas like the
Coke-head brother-in-law of the groom
he is. With no time to rehearse he kidnaps
the un-bride to the shrieking applause of
pre-teen boys and the scarlet
shame of fifty-six rows of adults
each with twelve seconds to choose.
Angst or relief or a sweeter choice
always around the ankles decisions gather
and only walking down the isle and out
will reveal the choosing
kind or violent, separating or joining with
all the doubt in the wide world.

Boychild

Twelve hours ago on her hands and knees, Emmy pushed an eight pound, seven ounce baby boy into this world. Ten minutes later a man in a white coat came in the room and said, "I'm sorry I missed the big event but my daughter had a school play and I turned my beeper off during her death scene." He sewed Emmy together, shook her boyfriend's hand, and wished them all happy Groundhog's Day before going to the parking lot and finding his black shiny car and driving to his house near the river. Later the good doctor will take a couple of xanax to take the edge off the day and make the night move a little more smoothly toward dawn.

After she offers her tender, swollen breast to her eager but awkward son, Emmy will accidentally look in the mirror and see her two blackened eyes, the bruises of bearing down so long, so hard. She will ask for something for the pain, the pressure between her legs that isn't going away. It has been thirty-two hours since she has slept and in four more her two teenaged daughters will be coming by to meet their brother. The nurse hesitates, says, "Well if you really think you need it. You could try a hot bath first or some tea. Or just hold that bundle and see if you still feel like complaining."

Toward daybreak the red baby boy will curl against Emmy's belly as she squirms for a comfortable position on the narrow bed. She is now that confusing, overwhelming combination of mama and food that will bond him to her until his friends see him holding her hand, swinging arms wildly in the mall. Then for years he will watch the deliberate distance between their bodies. As if she were the enemy or poison—proof of his pitiful dependence, his connection forever to softness, the playful color pink, and warm sweet milk.

Silent Road Trip

We drove and drove
we chose a path
we closed our eyes
and pointed west
or north
took all the wrong
turns.

We barely talked
sometimes I cried
you smoked and hummed
along to Cash, to Hank, to
Janice
all dead so long
now.

Leonard Cohn and
Willie and Merle
for Patsy's sake
we drive all night
after
midnight we walk
slow.

Stumble me home
tell me nothing
of your feather
bed or dry soul
word sweat
unsaid, uncried
truth.

Listening

You whispered
there's a dance south of the equator
you learned it in your Navy days
a rhythm with no past and no future
a place to rest your soul
a way to know for sure.

I leaned in, told you
I haven't believed in Latin America
since 1978, Kissinger and
Carolyn Forche never danced
or broke bread or lied to each other
and then we all fell apart together.

In a dip you say
we are all our own country now
make a flag, make a law
freedom is for sale and we bought it.
we'll raise our children to believe
in our ghosts and themselves.

I plead with the starlight
without my past I am too clean
without the future I have no need of wine
or god or these gloves
I am too light too silly too irrelevant
too free too alone.

At the bar I hear you say
to someone else
the tango is the key to immortality
the equator goes through every human heart
we all know the steps
come, leave your shoes.

I'll talk you through it.

Waiting

I read Hafiz
for comfort.
I read Hunter Thompson
to understand
why my son loves
him so.
Neither makes time
go quicker as
I wait for news.

My Father's Story

My father tells one story of his father. It goes like this:
He was a Northern Pacific brakeman. Not educated
enough to make engineer. He never hit me either.
Except that once. When I said, "Why should I listen to
you? You'll never hit me." Then his hard fist on my soft
seventeen-year-old face. Then I vomited and did what
he asked. I like my father in this story, his cocky
invincible teenaged voice. But I like my grandfather
more. His courage to contrast himself for the sake of his
soon-to-be-American-soldier son moves me, and I yearn
for his Low German lullabies and his bitter bohemian
whiskey served over brown sugar bread with cream. All
over before my father met my mother. I know from
snapshots that my grandfather grew prize-winning roses
and liked to have his hands on my grandmother, who
my father says beat the shit out of him regularly.

My Sister's Gun

There's a seat at the bar reserved for me because I was supposed to show up, because I was predictably thirsty, because I was raised Catholic and what we do—before, during, and after funerals and wakes, body visitations and rosaries and burial masses— is, we drink. We drink cheap wine and later whiskey. We tell the bartender to be generous. We are just coming from the undertaker. We picked out clothes and hymns and verses. Fill us up. We are cold. Fill us up. We still breathe. Fill us up. The dead would raise one if they could. I'm not hungry. I can't sleep. I forget if it's Tuesday or Friday or midnight. It's jazz, it's tuna fish hot dish, it's Folgers and Jell-O molds. Drink to get through this. Drink to remember. Drink to history and fiction blended into a blurry cocktail. My sister has forgotten most of it. Just last week, two decades later, she asks me if when we were cleaning out the house, did she claim a shotgun? Did she give her share of the ammunition to our brother? Or did she say no, take an extra piece of jewelry instead? Either way, now she wants a gun. She wants her gun, one of my father's or grandfather's. Smooth wooden shaft and cold hard trigger. She wants what she needs. This legacy. Men walking shelterbelts, boys shouting, a bottle of schnapps, a campfire, the smell of gunpowder and family. She wants to shoot her gun. She wants to learn how. She doesn't want to buy a pistol. She deserves her legacy of homicide and sixteen point antlers, a full bag, a pheasant in the cast iron Dutch oven, down jackets and camouflage and orange and walk for miles with this purpose, not an extra brooch or a sapphire ring, something blue to match my mother's dead eyes and her own. Eyes that didn't see the future that day, the coming need for sudden loud noises followed by blood.

A Certain Kind of Forgiveness-Part IV

My mother wants a new pair of shoes
slips off a suede loafer
slips her foot into
a new cognac colored
suede loafer
says to me
What do you think?
Do you like them?
My mother wants a new pair of shoes
she wants me to want them too
she wants me to believe
with her, that these shoes are
not just new,
but different.
I lie to her for the first time that day
tell her they are beautiful
unusual, special
just like her.
My mother eats me that day and
at the bottom of her stomach
my compass stops working.

When Lake Michigan Called

This crying, this mourning, this goodbye
you leaving, my staying
my secret list of things to burn
your reluctance to kiss me
tastes like black tea,
no honey, no milk
still I lean in, still you shudder
still I want to beg you, convince you
woo you, make my hometown
your hometown
when all along
we both know the Big Lake will win.
I regret turning my shoulder
to any bow
I walk along this river as
you drive to Lake Michigan,
a boat, a family waiting,
me finally on your list
of things to drown.

Lila, Hey

Toward all the love songs
I can't sing
and all the gods
you don't believe in,
we reached.

A heart too committed
to measuring
a heart afraid to rest
I wanted a sister
you wanted to run free.

Plants need water
hearts need songs
I need fast writing pens
edible cannabis
in my sock drawer.

We will be fine
we will be sorry
we will regret all this
we will make fire
and noise and bread.

Please Me

Please do not question my resolve for this much
freedom. Please do not turn off the music when I come
in the screen door, with our dog, with lilacs, with desire.

Please do not wonder if another chapter is coming.
Please do not convince me that you love me more than I
love you, silly, confusing, wishful.

Please do not ask me why I love baths and olive oil soap
and old-fashioned gospel played at high volume, robes
swaying, eyes closed against the wind.

Please do not call me before dawn asking for
reassurance or my quick laugh. Please do not think of
me at the alter or in the ocean or when you drink before
noon.

Please be kind when you tell my story—all my reasons
for loving you and all the excuses for leaving too. Please
hum my name as you walk toward her.

Voice Lessons

Words like orange juice, thick pulp in my teeth and
around the rim. Ascension, assumption, resurrection.
Sorrowful mysteries. Words like lace pinned to my
straight blonde hair, sliding down slowly, tugging at my
pink scalp, annunciation, transfiguration, salvation,
joyful mysteries. Day old caramel rolls. A greasy diner.
Daily bread, Hail Mary, a wedding at Cana, a boulder
rolled away in the night. One crown of thorns. Cut
grass, peonies on my grandmother's grave, that
shameless hussy of a flower. Hands, feet, piercings.
Luminous mystery. Station wagon running, waiting,
impatience, mortal or menial, bless me father for I have
sinned. Blessed fruit of a womb, whores, babies on the
river bank. I am not worthy to receive you.

Pale green glow in the dark. A string of beads in a
Christmas stocking. Fire in a tree, wind through the
wallpaper, love and fear are the same word. Bless me,
swear at me, worry over my soul. Too loud, too needy,
too silly. Original sin, longing, penance, my mother's gin
and tonic her voice full of vanity and sour martyrdom.
The hardest thing about having five daughters is keeping
the sheets white. Immaculate conception, resurrection.
Purgatory, lost souls, unbaptized babies, angel wings,
absolution without crucifixion. Kneeling, standing,
sitting, kneeling sitting standing. Pink robes, funny hats,
benediction, Franciscan, sacrament, forgiveness.

Honor him, honor her, pray to them, beg for
intercession. Cut myself, genuflect. Boyfriends,
girlfriends, queer and bisexual. Disco, butch, fem and
ambiguous and androgynous and fairies. Silk and linen.
Sacraments and sacrifice. Vows and epidurals and drunk
bridesmaids. Mortgage, reincarnation, tantra, the Dali
Lama and so many Marys. Girls should have girls.

Parenting theories and open marriage and gin with
everything. Lemon vodka, red meat, even Fridays.
Buried parents. Sunscreen and colonoscopies and green
tea and vitamin D and omega threes and bee pollen and
lavender and tai chi. Dorothy Parker and Gertrude Stein
and Susan Sontag and Alice Walker and Joy Harjo and
the jitterbug and my sweetheart's lap. Memorize this,
blessed virgin, holy moon phase, tarot and runes.
Kissing, missing, messy. Absolution, contrition,
contribution, reward and the bardo and the high dive
and soft landing, so near truth.

Acknowledgments

Perpetual thanks to my own circle of light: Adam Ratchenski, Lindsay Jones, and David Ratchenski. Also Carrie Carter, Kevin Zepper, Laurie Baker, and Rebecca Gardner.

Gratitude galore to the sisterhood plus one, Kathy, Mary Kay, Amy, Susy, and Joe and to the next generation, Cassie, Aly, Jaden, Katy, Justine, Emma, Andrew, Grant, Kolbie, Gavin, Ben, Josh, Andrea, Landon, Anna, and Adam—you are my hope for everything.

I am forever indebted to my clients who remind me daily, hour by hour, that love and creativity always light the way.

And deep thanks to my closest stars, Amy and Joe Kapaun. You are my favorite places in the world. Everything makes sense because you love me anyway.

Published Credits

"Boychild" and "My Father's Story" have both been published in Moorhead State University Minnesota's *Red Weather*. "Forgive This and That, Whatever" in the *Cider Press Review*, "Dying Stars" in both *Cutthroat 23rd edition for the Joy Harjo Poetry Competition 2018* and *DASH, Volume 11*.

About the Poet

Carol Kapaun Ratchenski is a lifelong resident of North Dakota, where you can see the sky without ever looking up and the open spaces demand art. And sometimes, love. Her first collection of poetry, *A Beautiful Hell*, won the 2016 Many Voices Project and was published by New Rivers Press. *A Beautiful Hell* has since been adapted to the stage by Laurie J. Baker with the support of Theater "B" and Humanities North Dakota. Ratchenski's first novel, *Mambaby* was published in 2013 by Knuckledown Press. Her work has appeared in *Gypsy Cab*, *Red Weather*, *North Dakota Quarterly*, *Wintercount*, *Lake Region Review*, *Dust and Fire*, *Dash*, *NDSU Magazine* and others as well as in the anthologies *Resurrecting Grace: Remembering Catholic Childhoods*, edited by Marilyn Sewell, Beacon Press, 2001, *The Cancer Poetry Project: Poems by Cancer Patients and Those Who Love Them*, edited by Karen B. Miller, Fairview Press, 2007, and *Visiting Bob: Poems Inspired by the Life and Work of Bob Dylan*, edited by Thom Tammaro and Alan Davis, New Rivers Press, 2018.

Ratchenski is a Licensed Professional Counselor and the owner/operator of Center for Compassion and Creativity in Fargo, ND, where she also lives. She is at work on a second novel while she prepares to be honest, loving, disruptive, and groovy at age sixty.

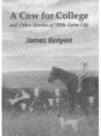

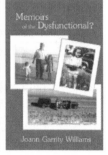

www.birdypoetryprize.com

Meadowlark Books created The Birdy Poetry Prize to celebrate the voices of this era. Cash prize, publication, and 50 copies awarded annually.

Entries Accepted: May 1 to December 1.

Final Deadline for Entries: December 1, midnight.

Entry Fee: $25

All entries will be considered for standard Meadowlark Books publishing contract offers, as well.

Full-length poetry manuscripts (55 page minimum) will be considered. Poems may be previously published in journals and/or anthologies, but not in full-length, single-author volumes. All poets are eligible to enter, regardless of publishing history.

See www.meadowlark-books for complete submission guidelines.

Made in the USA
Monee, IL
13 March 2020